T0132408

Everything You Didn't Want to Know about Sex

Somebody's got to Tell You!

Stuart Leamen

iUniverse, Inc.
New York   Bloomington

Everything You Didn't Want to Know about Sex
Somebody's got to Tell You!

Copyright © 2009 Stuart Leamen

All rights reserved. No part of this book may be used or reproduced by any means, graphic, electronic, or mechanical, including photocopying, recording, taping or by any information storage retrieval system without the written permission of the publisher except in the case of brief quotations embodied in critical articles and reviews.

iUniverse books may be ordered through booksellers or by contacting:

iUniverse
1663 Liberty Drive
Bloomington, IN 47403
www.iuniverse.com
1-800-Authors (1-800-288-4677)

Because of the dynamic nature of the Internet, any Web addresses or links contained in this book may have changed since publication and may no longer be valid. The views expressed in this work are solely those of the author and do not necessarily reflect the views of the publisher, and the publisher hereby disclaims any responsibility for them.

ISBN: 978-1-4401-7393-6 (pbk)
ISBN: 978-1-4401-7391-2 (cloth)
ISBN: 978-1-4401-7392-9 (ebook)

Printed in the United States of America

iUniverse rev. date: 9/23/09

Disclaimer:

This publication is intended as entertainment in the hopes that it will amuse and inform the reader. In some cases, this could help to illuminate a problem some couples might be experiencing and be means to start open conversation on a tough subject. Certainly, if there is a message, it is that you are very normal and whatever your situation, you have lots of company. I had well over one thousand conversations through chat, through e-mail, and over the telephone. Some of these subjects were in Europe and Australia. Only a fraction of these subjects were used. There are no subject names, user names, or Web sites named.

I would like to stress that a religious person is richer than one who's not. Any discussions of the Bible are interpretations of the author and simply reflect an opinion. There is nothing that claims we are godless, but the opinions cater to the idea of a spirit that is not defined literally by the Holy Bible.

A book of this nature would interest people who have a side of themselves that they are not so inclined to talk openly about. If nothing else, this book reveals that the desire for bizarre sexual activities is not that unusual, and many people are willing to talk about it. This book was written with limits; I received graphic descriptions of fantasies I could not bring myself to write, and I have not included them in this publication.

I stumbled onto these dating sites while Internet surfing, and these sites are available, in some cases, free of any charge. Curiosity provoked me to seek membership on a couple of these matchmaking sites. I found how varied these sites were, as to the extent of information available for anyone to examine. I joined and paid a fee for seven matchmaking Web sites and was given free membership on another four services. I ignored at least that many more that were anxious to have me join.

The instances described are altered only to hide the identities of those discussed. For instance the forty-year-old might have actually been fifty-five. The three-hundred-pound lady may have been four hundred pounds. Some minor alteration has been made to the description of each individual, but the activities described are accurate and presented to you, the reader, as this information was voluntarily given to me during phone calls, through private chat and e-mail, or by other means.

I used different user names on each site, and for my own profile I used a number of varying descriptions. I was as young as twenty-seven and as old as sixty-five. I was straight or bisexual or gay. I was into group activities or one-on-one. I was dominant or submissive. I was a male in every case.

Preface
by Reynaldo P. Olivia

This book comes from two years of touring Internet dating and matchmaking sites, gathering data about human sexual expression as well as taking a look into the lives of some that resort to emotional relief through e-mail or chatting with others who frequent such services.

When I started this project, I had other ideas of what I was going to do. I joined about eight matchmaking sites of various styles. There were many other sites I was able to view because some of these sites are free or give you a short-term membership to entice you to join them. With every site, I tested the waters and found different kinds of people with different features they were looking for in a mate. I have included some of the trials and tribulations of members of those more mundane pairing Web sites.

There is almost no story to be told of those simple matchmaking, well-known, well-advertised programs. You could say that their services are used by many people, and the sites do provide contacts that have made lots of people happy. Those businesses deliver a product that is honest and more or less live up to what they say they can do. However, to include much of what goes on as far as successes versus failures and frustration does not make for interesting reading.

The services that emphasize sex, on the other hand, include people from all walks of life and every level of education or income. The people are just like all of us and, like it or not, many people have an appetite for this. I have never been prudish, but with these sites, I felt prudish. I'm also trying to write this "potty mouth" free. You will note that the common dirty words are not used, though I must tell you they are nearly always used to express the pleasures people seek. They make it very clear, in very frank terms, what they want, how they want it, and what you are expected to deliver as a partner. Few are willing, however, to say too much on initial contact. You have to work on a trusting relationship and maintain a common interest in order to keep an exchange going. I have now e-mailed and chatted with and gathered information from a thousand subscribers, many who paid a fee to be a member in hopes of finding a lifelong partner.

Very often, no return is made. I would guess the ratio to be four to one against receiving a response. You never know how often a member visits one of these Web sites, as some do so frequently, even daily, and others once a week or even less often. I do think the Web sites lose members after bad contacts or dismal results and are not notified. So you could be e-mailing a ghost. When you become a member you are listed by the state and country and often by the city. Sometimes that has an unfavorable effect on responses as people are so far apart the connection becomes unlikely.

Membership fees vary and are designed to entice further spending and longer memberships. Some of these sites are very decent and have legitimate safety features and are trying to link people in a careful, sensible way. These sites are a little less interesting and will not embarrass you if somebody sneaks up behind you while you are cruising through candidates.

Then there are the other sites that are entertaining due to the content matter, which is definitely adult material. This book touches on some sensitive issues, which illustrate a point of view that may support an argument regarding the subject at hand. For instance, gay sex, religious discipline, and legalities are discussed, not to challenge any ideology, but as an observation of the effects of the philosophy on a given issue. For example, I consider threesomes to be a gay act for two of the participants, who might call that bisexual.

If you are a bisexual, you are one-half gay and one-half straight. That brings the genetics versus choice argument into question. You now have an idea of what direction this guide is going, and we can begin.

In my research, I would initiate contacts myself, as well as set up profiles to attract whomever I could. I started with a site that was pretty mild, and the profiles hinted but did not directly say anything at all. There appeared to be very lonely people hoping to make a connection with somebody. When that was the case I would be able to counter with some incompatible factor so as not to toy around with somebody's emotions. I would not exchange a chat or e-mail beyond an initial contact, and I would bow out gracefully. But the information that many of these folks provided is included in the data I recorded. Many of these people are socially timid ladies who are not willing to subject themselves to real-life situations.

With the tamer pairing services that loosely try to screen and weed out impostors, the women are seriously hoping to find their knight in shining armor. This seems to yield more disappointment or grief of other kinds. After a go-around with two or three prospects it became clear that the very best of the men may be few and far between on these dating services.

A man who turns to one of these Web sites may be looking over the pictures and choosing that way. When he makes a connection and conversation occurs, the guy may be looking to leap into a fast-moving relationship without a feeling-out process. When the lady expresses hesitancy, the guy's attitude will show his true impatience. This is a guy whose agenda is his way or the highway. It's my opinion, from the conversations I had with some of these women, that this is the most common type on these dating services.

The other common type of guy is a bad communicator who wavers with decisions regarding a first meeting or date. He often cancels, and this guy is probably afraid of rejection for any number of reasons, not the least of which being a lack of confidence in his appearance. The aggressive lady subscriber may be what is needed to bring about a face-to-face. Even an aggressive lady, after some of these episodes, may get frustrated and begin to question her own confidence. Making this work out will likely be a lengthy process; an instant connection is not the norm. A woman needs to be cautious and never get out of control early on in a relationship.

Most of the time, women end up losing confidence in the dating site as well because of these negative responses and controlling men who want to dictate where to meet. This is not the lady's idea of the way it should be, and this is a frequent and uncomfortable occurrence.

There are not a lot of early-twenties and teens on these Web sites. If they are younger, usually no prior marriage is mentioned. In general, we are talking about experienced women, many coming from a difficult former partner and not looking for another bad experience. The sooner a seriously searching man recognizes this, the sooner he will be rewarded when the lady finds him to be understanding of her situation. Too many assumptions are made, even before an initial meeting has occurred. The guy may be planning trips while the lady is looking for a coffee and discussion.

The largest number of women in this category are middle-aged and would find it uncomfortable to start dating again; they seem to find it intimidating, as younger women are everywhere. These profiles include different components that attempt to reveal what each member seeks.

Most male Internet surfers are seeking sex as a priority, and most females are seeking companionship. This is a basic observation and a rarely acknowledged difference among the human species. Most men want a sexual partner, for both one-time or regular visits, according to lady members.

You cannot run a dating Web site without at least a reference to the attitude of the member's sexual interest. One site uses a "turn-on" list, members who include things like "flirty" or "erotica," and a "turnoff" list, and finding "erotica" would likely reduce the number of contacts they receive from browsing men. Don't include it as a turnoff and don't use it as a turn-on. But the truth is, using it as a negative will produce negative results. This is a more ladylike way of expressing sexual interest or disinterest.

Then there are the middle-of-the-road dating sites, which will tolerate a stronger reference to the sexual attitude of the member. It is a little more revealing, as the lady expresses what romantic acts she likes and what might turn her on, or she might want a total lack of romance and emphasize companionship.

This will screen out men really looking for fun without having to work for it. This implies this member is a lady and wants to be treated as such. This does not have a completely negative effect, as seriously searching males will be interested in other parts of a new relationship. But there is a frankness there that could be a turnoff for men if the member strongly expresses that you need not apply if all you want is sex. That would be better left unsaid, as all men want that part in the romance.

So let's start with a lady who was obese and very hungry for sex. She was over three hundred pounds, and I think substantially over. She was a "switch" sexually, a term that indicates whether you like to be submissive or dominant. She would take either role. I decided to initiate contact and see if it would provoke a response. In her profile, she provided graphic images of her privates and reminded potentials they'd better like large women. I take on the mostly submissive male role.

We exchanged two brief e-mails that resulted in dialogue that I thought might go somewhere. Her language was quite graphic, and her expectations were spelled out. By about the fourth exchange, I could expound on what I would like, which was playing into the information she provided regarding what she did to excite herself. She then changed her attitude, telling me she needed somebody younger. I was sixty on this site.

I countered that age was not mentioned as an issue in her profile and that age is often a plus when seeking someone new. She said that she had no place to host me. I said I'd go wherever she wanted me to. As the communication continued, she requested pictures, which I took to mean her interest in me was increasing. The pictures can hurt a prospective encounter if the receiving party has an image in mind and you aren't that.

I don't believe being good-looking or not has that much to do with it. A picture was sent, and this lady approved. Her discussions became more inquiring. She enjoyed oral, anal, and vaginal penetration, but size was an issue because she is so large. She used props and had all she needed to perform light bondage with her as the dominant, and she described the sequence of how this prearranged activity should unfold.

I countered with what I would like to do and how I could "switch" with a partner's request. I could tell this lady was a little hungry, and the encounter might not work for me regarding her preference. Anal seemed most important to her, and I could have problems with that.

Also, organ size could be an issue; I am not sure what's too small or too large. I always thought myself to be average, and every man at least once put a tape measure to it and rounded off the fractions to the next-highest whole number. I am six inches by that formula, and that's at peak excitement. So now I didn't know if I was big enough for her to get the pleasure she sought. I was a little afraid to mention these issues; I wanted to see if I could get a date and place to meet.

This woman made it clear that looks were unimportant, and she related that she was three hundred pounds. Going by the picture she provided, I saw that she was not attractive! After I reluctantly sent a picture of myself, because I was trying to be as discreet as possible, the correspondence stopped. How bad am I if this woman, who struggles to get dates for sex and is not very appealing herself—but says looks don't matter—disses me after I send her my picture!

I also detected some moody periods when she felt comfortable with rude comments about my personality.

By far the most interesting of all the pairing sites are the SMBD pages. S is for sadism: willing to dole out physical pain for sexual pleasure. M is for masochism: willing to receive physical pain and humiliation for pleasure. B is for being bound and D, subjected to sexual discipline and domination. I profiled on an SMBD site that I thought could provide me with some insight into the hardcore players of this arena. Dominant females seem to offer lengthy recitations of their educational background and how this activity is furthering their study of this kind of human behavior. They usually announce what kind of slaves or submissives they are looking for and literally are into their roles as they write their profiles, which made me think they were getting some pleasure out of describing who could or could not approach them.

I found practices and language and visuals on these sites that would dictate some caution. One might think some of these people are sad and pathetic, but frankly, I don't think so at all. I believe these sexual urges have been around awhile, and people with them have finally seen something that might bring such fantasies to reality. As there are a lot of older folks, I think that age plays into the situation, as people might feel that time is running out for them to do some of these things. Or they may have lost a partner, and there is not a lot out there for pairing old-timers. Particularly so if their sex is driven by nontraditional activities.

Submissives, males and females, are by a long shot more available. Our human sexual preference is to be used, and a submissive does not have too many boundaries. I would say a sub is risking injury with some of these slave masters. I have e-mailed several of these seemingly strong doms.

I provided for this site a picture of a sub male, pretty available for anything and asking what to do to get involved with someone when I send an e-mail.

The first one replied snottily that she didn't deal with subs; she has slaves, "Good day!"

I was dismissed, and I knew I was going to have to have somebody explain the difference between a willing sub and a slave. A dom with an arrogant attitude is more common than a cordial one. It had become abundantly clear this is a closed society, and cracking into servicing is tricky.

I made another humble inquiry to a middle-aged dom with a shaved head, who unmistakably objected to the fact that I wrote her at all. This confused me because the site's purpose, I thought, was to put people together for sexual oddities because it's difficult to find the right person to openly ask about them!

I was given no worthwhile information, and so I portrayed myself as exactly what she was seeking in obedient subordinate men. She wanted slaves that she could not only punish, humiliate, leash, beat, and restrain them naked to satisfy her sadistic desires, but also slaves to do her housework, from dishes to laundry to vacuuming.

She provided pictures of primarily white guys, chained, with serious red welts on their backsides. And her profile, an endless composition of million-dollar words, made it clear she got off on destroying white men younger than she was, and her total snub of me was, I believe, because of the sixty-year-old factor. Maybe she was afraid she'd kill me! So with this dom I was to never able to receive the slightest return of interest in me, even though I might have been the perfect slave for her; she looked scary.

I continued on this path to create a dialogue with the doms. I attempted to get exchanges from a young, twenty-three-year-old who suggested in her profile that she would take on all parties willing to let her do whatever she wanted. I sent her an e-mail stating that I had some experience and was regarded by my doms as highly obedient and a great submissive. I told her that the more dominant, the hotter I got, and nothing requested would be too much for me to handle. I received an auto response that she was very busy but would respond soon.

After two weeks with no response, I did not expect to hear from her. I continued to try to draw somebody into conversation who would offer me a date. I tried a woman in her midforties who claimed to be the best of her specialty, and she did not have subs but slaves. I still had not figured out the differences between them.

My imagination always centered on a male who got greater arousal from subjecting himself to the humiliating and often painful actions of doms, who get arousal from controlling a man and having freedom to do anything she wants to the willing male, who puts himself in a position not to be able to stop her. It was clear that dominating ladies liked issuing punishment to obedient men without any further physical contact.

I could not create a better grouping of words to offer the advertising dom to provide her with exactly what she wanted. I received no response, and I could not tell if she checked out my profile, which gave her all those things she seemed to stress as the qualities needed to serve her.

Then there were the duo doms, who were very sharp-tongued and could excite a reader. These two were experienced older women. They made it clear that after humbling their subordinates, they would become tools of their own pleasures if they chose. A candidate would be tested to be worthy of their brand of humiliation, which included exposure to other guests during your training, who would observe you servicing these prima donna doms! I e-mailed them a most enticing description of a past experience that included some origination of service and a willing S&M subject, including many of the fetishes so often listed. This drew no response. My goal was to provide myself as a candidate, and yet I was nearly striking out with them all! I received no reply. I would go as far as a face-to-face meeting before backing out, and backing out was my intention, for the purposes of writing this book.

It's clear to me some of the problems subscribers encounter is not knowing how long an interesting-looking match may have been on the site, or whether that party doesn't bother checking very often, waiting for the membership to terminate. There are other problems, but most of them are generated by the members and not the Web site's rules. There was also what I believe was a counterprogressive feature of the Web site that turned me off. Sites claim that interested parties are waiting for your response, but upgrading your membership is required to see them. I consider that a clear rip-off and an absolute reason for me not to extend a membership.

Some of these sites have a hold on new members; they provide a view of profiles and then tell new members that better and more costly kinds of memberships get at them first. And often these new members seem to disappear after a few days and are never heard from again.

I do not provide a picture, which does limit visitors to your profile. However, it's difficult to remain discreet while providing an accurate photo of yourself. There is a heavy emphasis on discretion—it may be the most frequently used term among users.

Some of the sex sites are very revealing in both pictures and text. I experimented with the text end of it, playing into the stated desires of the advertising member. A dom would be very demanding of obedient slaves and submissives, and I would answer with a torrid explanation of how those desires make a connection with me perfect. Most of the time, I received no responses!

Very often a dominant or submissive would emphatically say looks were not a consideration because sometimes bad looks make it all the more exciting. For instance, large women are much more enticing in the female dominant role, to add realism to the situation. Real masochists prefer their doms to be physically able to handle them, and a capable sadist would have the physical ability to handle her submissive. Otherwise the realism is reduced and the fantasy is less gratifying. This kind of sexual preference is very common and widespread in both sexes.

One could argue that statistics from these dating Web sites, some sexual in nature, would present skewed results in trying to compare it to the general population. If you read the information carefully, you discover these are normal people, working normal jobs, with very common sexual desires.

You can't argue that they are not typical because they indulge in these Internet dating services. Although there is a hint of desperation in some participants, the majority seem to be reaching out for more involvement with people of whom they are not afraid to request activities that they might be embarrassed to ask of their life partners.

There is a link in my findings between religious conviction and extent of involvement. It's clear that religious upbringing made sexual discussion and activity limited, as the Christian and Jewish faiths appear to be less than enthusiastic for anything other than procreation.

In fact, the Bible repeatedly condemns sex in anything other than straight married couples for purposes of babies; the idea of pleasure is condemned. There is no doubt that if reproduction did not occur through intercourse and the regeneration of life was the random release of sperm in areas of random eggs, like fish, there would never have been an occasion for male or female interaction to be okayed by the writers of religious scripture. In American life, which has historically trumpeted its Christian values, it appears that rebuking the churches' point of view is well underway.

This is not a discussion of the merits of religious value; it's an observation that the views of Americans who grew up influenced by parents and clergy are being discarded by many who, prior to these times, would have been afraid to practice anything contradictory to church doctrine. This does bring up the question of how much damage the church may have inflicted through its self-serving dictate of restraint for sexual activities. No, they cannot credibly defend their doctrines in this regard, as the activities of the clergy themselves suggest major fraud. The Bible even contradicts itself by relating many of the heroes' sexual adventures and the instances of polygamy and mentions of concubines.

The suppression of natural and instinctive human desires has resulted in a screwed-up social understanding of where you should be, sexually speaking. The ability of man to produce thousands of offspring and maintain sexual interest throughout most of his life speaks to a dirty cruel trick of God, if it's his intention to only allow copulation for procreation.

By all natural evidence, sexual desire was a gift from nature or God. Sex is to be a pleasure and not a shameful act! There is no doubt that generations up to now have had guilt drummed into their heads about this matter. The repression and coping with that repression is a danger to domestic relations and to the health of an individual's sex life. Historically, it appears the church has not practiced what it preaches. There is much more supporting evidence that the reason many hold back, particularly females, is their religious upbringing. Instead, this should be a strictly moral issue, and each adult should be able to decide their own moral point of view.

I do not know whether evolution or divine intervention is the origin of life, but I'm sure the sex drive would have been more controlled if God's intentions were to be so restricted. This is not to advocate that all do whatever they want; protection from unwanted sex is always the standard.

Adult human beings should not face condemnation for this human expression; it is a gift and perhaps the absolute best gift when unbridled between willing participants. Consenting adults should by all reason be able to do what they want. Sexual activity is wonderful and most wonderful when each party has no drummed-in guilt of what is okay or not okay to do. The standard measure should be the level of satisfaction each party reaches, and one partner returning the favor for another would be the reward.

There is a tremendous amount of sexual dissatisfaction as shown on some of these matchmaking Web sites. Some of these activities are downright embarrassing to hear of, but at the same time, having a place to attempt to bring these fantasy/fetishes to reality is more healthy than suppression to the point of committing a crime or destroying a relationship.

It is interesting to consider other species and their sexual habits, which are not dictated by religious or moral considerations. There is a reproductive process for all living things, and it seems the higher the form of life, the higher the levels of courtship and choice in partners. None of those other species deny themselves of these pleasures. A wildebeest or porpoise does what comes naturally. There are no rulebook-dictated considerations. And the animal world seems to know that naturally!

As a rule, getting a lot of dialogue from people proclaiming to be specialists, shall we say, is not common. They are guarded with their commentary, other than what is posted on their profile. So you have to make contact and do something to capture their attention.

A dominant female in her early twenties interested me, as she looked a little young to be as advanced in this activity as her profile indicated. I managed to pose as a potential slave, and got a lot of feedback from her. She was college educated and held a master's degree. She was able to provide visuals of her chamber of obedience, with various props, their purposes unmistakable.

Oftentimes, a female dom would make it clear that no sexual contact was guaranteed, as the excitement they could create plays into denying the slave any pleasure beyond the discipline. It appeared that this type of mistress would go as far as she could for arousal and walk away pleased at having left the man helplessly awaiting satisfaction.

This particular woman started to be graphic; I think she was interested in securing a visit from me because of what she knew about me—some college education and a midmanagement position in an important occupation. She knew my physical size, which was double hers in weight. I pretended to be what I thought she was looking for, which was a man to idolize her and be militarily obedient to any of her many whims.

Her scene was making a man get to his peak excitement, abusing him to the point of unshackling him and leaving him on the floor of the studio, and demanding that he leave. She would not return. She looked for clients that would find that what they wanted, and these clients would in fact return time and time again for that style of sex. She did not want young men and stated that experience in this activity was preferred. She liked middle-aged or older and totally submissive clients. She said that after the person would leave, she would relive the event in her mind and pleasure herself, who, she explained, was the only one who could know what to do.

She had tables outfitted with ankle- and handcuffs and a circular rack, to stretch a body. She had a bar with ankle shackles that allowed her to suspend an individual upside down and various whips, straps, and strap-on devices. She also liked women her age and up to thirty years old for bondage and submissive activity. She claimed her only sexual contact would more likely be with women, but her greatest highs were seeing the unsatisfied men lying on the floor as she walked away. There appeared to be a number of the female doms that had profiles that led me to believe the scenario of male arousal and then denial was not uncommon.

There was another lady, who was looking for men over forty to diaper. She boasted that she's diapered hundreds of men over the years and implied that it is the guy with that fetish and she is a pro. At my age, I still like the idea that I'm not in need of that yet!

I tried to make conversation with her by implying an interest in her service. About the third time I sent an e-mail, I got a response. I said I'd never have had that experience but it sounded hot.

She said no one can bring a man to climax without having technique and strength. She went onto say she was fifty years old and big enough to handle a two-hundred-pound man the way he wants to be handled as she performs the diaper change. She referred to her clients as "babies." She also said she did not get involved with sexual contact, but with the right "baby," she could lactate and would let him suckle. She had converted a space in her home to handle very big babies, with a changing table and a playpen.

She provided me with photos that showed her holding a subject up by his feet as she powdered a bare behind. She also cradled in her arms a small-framed male, holding him to her ample chest, and he was on her nipple. She implied her clients would come and go throughout the past nine years, and I believe she made it clear that clients treated her very well for this not-so-common service.

I asked how long a session was and what made up a session. She said an hour with her baby was ample enough time and that most of her clients reached satisfaction somewhere through her routine, and oftentimes that was less than fifteen minutes. I asked her for a reference, hoping I could get away with it and she wouldn't detect my fading enthusiasm to show up there, as she was pushing for an appointment.

To my surprise I got someone and now had to persuade him that I was a prospect for the service. This guy turned out to be a professor at a well-reputed university. He was middle-aged and beyond my level of intelligence. He'd been going once a month for two years, and most of the time he cannot get off any other way, including masturbation. He was into role-playing and he enjoyed being an uncooperative child that had to be spanked into behaving for the diaper bit.

I asked for the scenario and his was to be set in his briefs in the playpen until she came in. She's big enough to lift him out of the pen and put him across her lap while removing his underwear at which point he starts to fight her and squirm. Of course she's allowed to overpower him, and she places him on the gigantic changing table, where she manhandles him into an adult diaper. The woman did not impede clients handling themselves, as a client who could satisfy himself put an end to the session more quickly and she would watch him masturbate, which added, according to the gentleman, to the excitement. A tip is routine. I think Americans, in particular, are very hung up about sex in general and fetishes are embarrassing to them, even though there is a world out there with a different point of view.

The pee-on-me fetish is not unique. These are usually women who express a desire to be in a men's restroom and be a choice, next to standing and seated appliances, for men to pee in. I found this fetish request several times. They wanted to be stripped and made to kneel, for height convenience, and simply be peed upon on any part of their body, usually preferring in their mouth.

The two that I attempted communication with seemed uninterested in consuming the urine, just having it flow on or over and orally in them and flow off them. No sexual contact in this act. Men were supposed to just step up to the woman as if she were a human urinal. I tried communication and suggested their fantasy had some obstacles to be overcome.

The strategy to make this work could become difficult as placing one's penis in someone's mouth would cause a reaction that would make it hard for a guy to go. Maybe older men that have been using urinary-assist drugs are a market for their users as they impede erection sometimes and semen all the time. The other problem is that the woman would be naked with excited men but she would not want sexual contact beyond the peeing event. Not a well-controlled situation.

One of these ladies responded rather snottily because I was damaging her fantasy. But I don't see how a normal guy could stick his member in her mouth and still remain flaccid and be able to urinate. And we're talking about a row of these kinds of guys.

You know, one might think a group of gay guys would be able to do so, but I am pretty sure any sober man would be aroused by this activity. I asked some of the people on this Web site if they'd ever taken part in something like this. I asked about my thought of the difficulty that would be hard to overcome and found no one in disagreement with me. I did not find anyone who had participated in something like this as a group. This may be one of the most bizarre of fetishes, but I cannot tell you how often the same fantasy was expressed by women of various ages all over the United States.

It is not that easy to obtain responses from candidates for various partnerships. You may have to send some form of communication a dozen times to someone, and you're always wondering what will attract a response. So you play to their descriptions in their profile. If the lady wants to be someone's slave, you offer in no uncertain terms that you can be a master and would see that she did all that you wanted, by threat of punishment. This has never gotten a response. People offering to be subs are afraid to communicate with somebody offering the master role. Most often, the description states that they would serve any walking being.

Next, I dabbled on a gay site and actually found responders for subs and one scary response from a dom who clearly enjoyed fetishes I would find unappealing. This one dominant male was the equivalent of the diaper-changing woman. He wasn't interested in diaper changing but in cross-dressing and then dressing partners like girls. He was, by his description, six foot five and 350 pounds and could handle willing male partners like they were children. He had a picture of himself and he was not good-looking, but I'm not sure that that was a hindrance, as ugliness might have played into the excitement of the experience.

He said he would only host you at his home, and the features in the background of a picture he provided looked like he was seriously into his pleasures. I wondered if that region had disappearing men on occasion. He offered a cell phone number, and I did call it and pretend to be an interested party. I sensed he was a person who knew what he was doing, and that he was not in fact a danger but may have been something less than the brightest bulb on the tree.

And our conversation went like this: "I read your profile, and it excites me!"

He responded boldly, "That's good; let me tell you what I like to do."

I replied, "Okay."

He then said, "When you come in, you are mine to do whatever I want with, but I don't hurt anyone. But you will be unable to get away from me, and when I'm excited, you can't turn me back."

Then he asked how big I am, height and weight. I am big enough to be at least formidable in a scramble for survival, so I tell him I'm big enough to take care of myself.

That ended it! He said he was not interested then!

The female "doms" did not seem threatening, merely role playing.

This specific male "dom" offered that once you agree to be a partner and he is into his role and is aroused, it wouldn't be easy to stop the activity. To me that suggests "caution".

I am suggesting you assess the risk possibilities with the "dom" you pick.

I did not feel seriously threatened by any of the female "doms" I talked to.

So what are these "smutty" pairings all about? This is sex, and to describe it as not being sex because there is no participation or penetration is baloney. You have to be out of the room, at least, to claim you are not taking part. Observing a nonpublic display of exposed male or female body parts makes you a participant. If you are touching anyone who is exposed, even though it may be in a manner in which a sex act is not occurring, it still makes you a participant. If you are a master or dom who is attending a submissive and expose his or her body parts, you are participating in a sexual situation.

The fifty states have laws that apply to some of these acts, making them illegal if an arresting authority wants to pursue it. However, I would agree that consenting parties of adult age and sound mind ought to be able to do these things without penalties of law. I say this because, contrary to the public point of view regarding morals and decency, most people enjoy or wish to enjoy the activity that excites them, and the numbers of people involved indicate that normal human beings have these ideas of sexual pleasures. Fetishes are numerous and involve all kinds of things. Humiliation and pain are major issues, and sometimes you can see the excitement of the party in his or her facial expressions.

Sex has three primary motivations: love, fun, and business. "Love" is the sexual experience for people falling in love or people who believe they're falling in love. This is not exclusively for young people, and many times the experience of sincere love could be repeated in a lifetime. Some people will tell you this is the absolute best reason for sexual involvement with somebody, that emotions flow simultaneously with sexual feelings, resulting in the most pleasurable sex. I certainly felt that for myself and believed it to be rewarding sex, and for a number of years I had those emotional climatic experiences. Very rarely, I suspect, does this feeling go on forever in a monogamous relationship. The excitement often dwindles after years in such a relationship, sexually speaking. It is rare that a couple stays as sexually active and equally satisfied as the years add up, but it is very good when it happens.

I think excitement dwindles for reasons unavoidable. The regularity and familiarity causes a natural decline of the excitement for many people. This only has to occur with one member of a couple for the other to suffer the effects. So to have two partners at the top of their sexual and emotional excitement forever is unrealistic. I should mention that this all has to do with aging and the various mental and physical aspects that causes less intimacy.

Married couples usually marry because they are in love, with the normal marriage life producing trials and tribulations as well as families.

During those continuing years the frequency of sex declines and the actions become routine. That tends to diminish the pleasures for both partners and it is not a subject often discussed beyond the frequency issue.

The important parts, for instance what might turn someone onto a greater orgasm, has this ingrained idea of it being embarrassing, does not get discussed, and this could be a potential infidelity problem.

Monogamy, whether married or not, causes their sex acts to be so familiar that the drive is of less interest and the couple seldom discuss the problem.

It has left many of the married couples that had a very good start in life, when love sex was going on and the heights of its pleasures were being enjoyed. For continued satisfying sex, the couple has to know each other well enough to communicate what works and does not work to keep their sex interesting. The driving force behind sexual excitement is what feels best for anyone. Sometimes straight couples do not enjoy traditional intercourse as much as oral stimulation, and I dare say that the percentage of people with that preference may be higher than 95 percent. People will do what is most exciting or satisfying. Sexual pleasures are mostly if not entirely physical. There are emotional experiences for many, but the one constant is physical pleasure. A primary reason divorce occurs is because someone is unfaithful, and that may have much to do with the lost excitement with sex. Today there is a large market for sexual enhancing drugs that help somewhat. The advertisements for these drugs say that what you've just read is pretty much fact. Aging, for one reason or another, takes its toll on couples with a long married life, often causing the sex to go sour.

The spice that gives a lift, literally and physically, is a different partner. A different partner that you need not marry or live with. Just the different body, of any shape and of a functional age, will bring a legitimate boner back or start the lady juices flowing. Now, deciding to stray has its complications, and discretion is my advice for anybody doing or considering doing it.

I say, with all sincerity, that a society that fosters acceptance of these situations has a lot fewer complications involving marriage. But it takes two partners, carefully assessing the health of a continued partnership while one or both partners seek sexual gratification with other people. There are many mature couples that have for some time had a healthy marriage but different sex partners. It takes a turn away from traditional values and stretches emotions, but it is workable to love your spouse while having a sexually satisfying experience with someone else. It defies only a tradition or value instilled in you. This is not a religious or moral consideration, and if you already know that it is a moral consideration for you, then it is not a solution for you!

The "fun" motivation involves, in the twenty-first century, most younger and unmarried people enjoying the social acceptance of sex and the expectation that sex will occur with some couples for fun and some for mistaken love. This has now beaten back some of the religious taboos and morals to become an individual issue, and parents are less and less involved with those decisions. It is also a reason for people who are not remaining monogamous or for more mature people who are dating to have sex.

So fun is the primary reason such "smut" pairing services can boast millions of members worldwide. It would not be a good idea to get involved with a participant on such a Web site if love is on your mind; I think the ratio is very high for people on these sites who are not looking for love in the traditional sense. The fetish sites are full of people who are not looking to be romanced with a dinner and movie, to be followed by a bedroom encounter of passionate sexual intercourse. Neither the dinner, the movie, nor the intercourse is what's being sought there.

In the fetish category are some really mind boggling ideas of sexual excitement.

Not very often talked about are practices that come very close to serious injury and sometimes death.

As mentioned before there seems to be more servitude preferred for sexual arousal than to be the one doling out the discipline.

Along this line of wanting to be dominated is the extent of tolerance of pain or pretend pain.

One of the common kinds of this activity is the practice of simulated strangulation during sex play.

It is more implied in public than is recognized.

One popular TV series has had scenarios where this may have been the reason for the dead body.

These practices can be fantasized or actually acted out with or without a partner.

The connection between erotic pleasure and near death experience are in unexpected places and you may not recognize it is occurring.

I saw a film that was either staged or for real, I thought for real, where a famous very large wrestler took on a lesser known but still professional boxer. The purpose was to see who would win a fight between the different styles of fighting.

Two big men in a fight for real to produce bragging rights to who is tougher, a boxer or a wrestler.

The first two minutes the boxer hit the wrestler mercilessly with a barrage of punches that prevented the wrestler from doing anything but covering himself up.

But he wasn't getting hurt.

After the boxer punched himself out of breath and realized his punching was doing no damage, he was in retreat!

When the wrestler was able to get hold of the boxer it was quickly over as the wrestler picked up this opponent and basically held him high off the ground in a "backbreaker" position, rendered the fighter to a "rag doll," and carried his captured prey around the ring for several minutes to illustrate his dominance.

It became embarrassingly clear that the boxer, being helpless in the big man's grasp and being carted from one corner of the ring to the other was becoming aroused over it.

It was clearly visible and quite apparent to everyone but the wrestler as this vision lasted longer than it should have.

Emergency responders can tell you about "untimely" death calls that appear to be suicides with some senseless clues at the scene indicate something different than a suicide.

Very often suicides involve naked victims, a factor that, for lots of years, confused responders because of the frequency of this occurring.

The scene of a hanging nude man is common enough to have a term for it which makes reference to holding off an orgasm while limiting the flow of oxygen until the very last second.

In some of these cases, the oxygen flow is held off too long and an accidental death occurs. This is not a suicide. It's risky behavior gone too far.

Often objects are found about the body like ropes around the neck and genetials as this can enhance the orgasm of masturbation. This practice can be used by one's self or with a partner. This is nearly an exclusively involving men and never women. It's called "auto-erotic asphyxiation."

Another one of those notable differences between men and women sexually.

I stumbled across a "spanker," who offered a treatment similar to our lady who diapered men. He wanted to spank and punish bare-bottomed men. He claimed little sexual contact but listed about every kind of fetish or sexual activity possible. This guy was forty-five and supplied a picture of him spanking the behind of an adult with his pants around his ankles.

Some or most of these sites offer several pictures. This man's next picture showed a naked man suspended by his feet on some metal contraption and the host wailing away with a paddle, reddening the man's buttocks substantially. This guy practiced sadistic sexual activities and advertised no contact. You might think about that before succumbing to those urges that might move you to him. That suspended fellow, by the picture, hardly looked like he had any control of the situation, but not having control and being abused play to the pleasures of a masochist. Like some of the others fetishes, there were lots of people into this!

I can tell you that emergency rooms, police departments, and emergency medical technicians have treated some odd injuries and people who were in a bind. Whether it be a male or female that gets aroused by sadistic acts, he or she is going to get heightened excitement from the more realistic pain they inflict, and the more their victim reacts, the intensity can increase to the point where there is a danger of not recognizing an injury. I have read of a man being crushed to death by an obese woman who mistakenly thought the victim's scream for help and for her to get off of him were part of the act. That is a manslaughter charge, providing it was consensual.

Men like a certain equality or even superiority in physical and sometimes rough sex play. In these dating services, there are questions that indicate the style of sex, and "like it a little rough" far outnumbers the mentions of "soft and tender"! I have from time to time conversed with ladies, aged forty and over, whom I know well enough to ask this, and it's at least four out of five who want it a little rough and want a man to manhandle them. Even a little hurt is sometimes smirked back at me.

Most ladies said they liked it a little rough and implied both ways, giving it and receiving it. "Smirky" is how I imagined or sensed their attitudes toward the subject.

Money does make its subtle appearances in these communications. The Web site owners seem to look to reduce or eliminate members who treat it as a "business" for continued membership. Any kind of monetary reward being solicited for is illegal most everywhere in the United States. I should point out that a member implying that money is expected for service is an equal crime to a responding member agreeing to pay. But I have had payment clearly implied with as many fetish practitioners as I didn't.

An implication that money or rewards of value were expected prompted the end of my communication with a person, and I would respond that my interest was for the height of sexual enjoyment and the involvement of money made us not at all compatible. My sex partner's only motivation should be the same as mine. No truer statement can be made in this regard, as a time element will be induced and a person thinking of profit is not going to be led into vigorous sex-driven actions. That partner is not going all the way to maximize sexual pleasure, and I don't want a letdown at my expense.

I had been corresponding with a young woman dom who so far had done everything interestingly right. Now, I admit I have my own idea of what I think would be the way I would want a dom to work. This lady had a look that was attractive and sexy, and she had a toughness from the mean streets. She demanded obedience, as many do, to some attitude of great arrogance, which is part of the game. She replied with a verbal onslaught of insults intended to make you feel subservient to her. Her terms are unique; she seeks to verbally humiliate you: "On your knees, you scum of the earth!" I think she wants to see how you respond so she can detect if you're in the spirit and a good candidate. There was no monetary reference after about four exchanges, so I pressed forward to try to see how real she was.

The quintessential female dom to me is one who is capable of actually instilling fear without the real threat of pain and who can drive you to the maximum of what she properly assesses you find most satisfying. This process could not happen with just a couple of verbal exchanges; I would need to test my responses. I tried to respond with what I thought she wanted to hear, with a great deal of humility. If she stopped responding or delivered an unmistakable "Don't talk to me again," I'll know I'm a poor candidate for a real hard-core lady dom.

The one thing missing from what I believe a dominant women needs is the strength to control certain physical maneuvers that would excite the client. The reality is a dominant female needs some superior abilities to make a wavering client fall in line.

On the other hand, it is not too difficult for a woman seeking a male dom, as he will have planned some restraint and binding and very compromising positions for her that he likely could physically do. The lady seeking a stronger male dom is involved with some risk, but I am sure most male doms' ultimate goal is a satisfactory climax through his dominance being forced on a willing lady. If there ever was a place for a person with evil intentions, this cannot prevent that risk. A larger dominant can do his or her will in some cases, even after you've changed your mind about the activity. Having no place to escape should be avoided. I know females are capable of the same kind of excitement from fetish activities, but they should know that turning back an excited, large, dominating male could be dangerous. The same is true for a gay couple of either gender practicing SMBD.

I had been corresponding with a twenty-two-year-old female dominant who was a senior in a highly respectable college. I found myself groveling to get her to respond. She interested me because of the language she used in self-promotion—what she expected and what could eliminate you on your first attempt to talk to her. She was very explicit that you should not expect sex, but you should expect discipline and consequences if you couldn't deliver yourself to her completely. I got her to respond, and she hurled back at me what a lowlife she thought I was already. She told me I didn't deserve a sniff at any body part of hers from what she had heard from me so far. It was of course questionable as to whether she was soliciting a response from that comment or wanted me to hit the road because she was not interested.

So I returned a beg of forgiveness and included a humiliating offer that I didn't think was crossing the line yet. Her response, I believed, was to test whether I was a true subservient or somebody soliciting an opportunity for a sexual experience with a pretty, young coed. Some time passed, and I thought she was gone. I guessed I hadn't given the right response to spark her interest in me as a candidate for her style.

After a week, this young dom sent another message, calling me unworthy again and telling me that any more disobedience would call for her to sever all communications. So now I was trying to assess what she was looking for. I apologized and asked what I had done, and I said that if I had done something disrespectful, I was sorry and at her disposal, prepared to face the consequences. She came back with an explicit comment involving my tongue. I offered a willingness to do it. I did not think I had given her enough to continue, that my imagination would not measure up to hers. There are, as I realized, graduated levels of disgust and humiliation designed to titillate and maintain interest.

She then returned with the common humiliation idea of putting your sub on a collar and leash; she expected an unlimited amount of time with me, and I was to expect to perform nonsexual chores at her home. She told me that I needed to give her all control and surrender my clothes at the door and they would not be returned until she got ready. I had not decided what to do with this young dom for whom I was, it appears, of interest as a potential submissive subject.

I would like to know how secure these women actually are who can subject themselves to an unknown subject. So far, most of the dominant women appear to be of high intelligence and must be prepared for an unwanted visitor or an invited visitor going bad.

The picture people provide is not necessarily valid, and it is really difficult to verify a person's looks, particularly if that party is hiding it. So I don't know if the picture of the lady is authentic, and I do not know if there is strong protection for her in the environment she's inviting me into.

Whether she will be alone at the rendezvous place can be found out by carefully reading the information she provided on the dating Web site. Sometimes the subject will mention other clients being around, and that means it is possible she will not be alone should you meet.

I have observed that rendezvous places and actual addresses are often public and rarely private homes. There are lots of reasons for that: privacy and security are risked because of observing neighbors and regular happenings around the house, such as the mailman or Aunt Louise dropping by. Clubs and bars seem to be a favorite meeting place, and why not? If anyone questions you, you are simply there for a drink. But I think making some arrangement with the club manager to ensure your safety should also be in place. I would further suggest that if you are invited to a session in that rather commercial environment, there are security, cameras, and audio devices somewhere. I'm not suggesting that risk is the only concern. The idea of remaining discreet is also at risk.

If I had some say in the meeting location, it would be at a mutually agreed-upon motel where the parties each could drive themselves to, at a location where the parties involved were unlikely to be known. The other reason to drive by yourself is for escaping purposes, should it reach a point where you would want to.

As far as my young coed friend would go, I wouldn't go to the address provided. I didn't know what kind of property it was, and the turf would have been hers, and she had already informed me that my clothing would be under her control. You are not going to escape easily naked! The only clue I had of her was a reference to other submissive clients, and it is not made clear whether you would be alone. One line in the information about her sounded like she did or could handle more than one sub at once. Now this could have been a ploy to generate more excitement for parties involved or a way for the dom to produce a greater reward for herself. I decided to try to take this a step further, if communication continued, to an alternate site, using the "equal playing ground" argument.

Another interesting member on my search was advertised as another spanker of bare-bottomed men. This one, however, was a woman claiming to be fifty-nine. The pictures provided showed a normal-looking senior woman in an ordinary, older, ladylike dress. There was another picture of her, with an adult man bent over her knees with very reddened buttocks while she was hanging onto a hairbrush. There was still another picture, of a wall where paddles of varying sizes hung. In this picture, another man was standing but bent over, pants on the floor around his ankles, and she appeared to be wailing away on him. She explained the role she played was the mommy with a bad little boy, whose pants she pulled down and spanked until enough pain was expressed. She further suggested that she had brought tears to her subjects' eyes. She sounded enthusiastic about what she did. She also claimed she was not involved in anything but spanking and that this is not a sexual act.

The facts are that pain, real and pretended, can cause arousal, and the S&M industry is flourishing greater today than ever before. It is indeed a common sexual activity, and I do not belittle anyone enjoying that. If kept quiet and away from children, these kinds of activities will grow, given the state of ever-decreasing moral regards. I hope laws are not created to limit this adult activity.

I tried to get some dialogue going with this elder veteran of strange professions. Again, you have to guess what you might say to stand out enough to receive a response. I told her I loved the pain, that her seniority to me would psychologically bring me to a climax rather quickly, and that it just sounded so hot. The idea of an elder women having me in a position that she could do to me what she wanted was a little bit more exciting. I hoped that resonated with her feelings also.

She responded in a fairly short amount of time, within two days, and that is quick for this medium. She then told me she could guarantee satisfaction, as she continues spanking until she observes an erection. Older men often had fifteen-minute sessions, and even if an erection did not occur, ejaculation of some degree would eventually.

I told her she sounded very experienced and pressed for more comments. I asked her how she could tell if someone was getting excited, as her view would be limited. She responded that she checked by feeling from time to time for an erection, either on her lap or by reaching down to touch the man. Sometimes her first touch would initiate an orgasm very quickly. She said she has never spanked anyone only once, other than first timers!

It is interesting that the portly ladies have no difficulty attracting men. It seems an exaggerated myth is that fat women are not sexy. I believe you have a bigger chance of being nonsexy if you are very slim. There are many women that make it clear they are bigger and if you don't like bigger, move on. There does not appear to be any advertising of thinness with gusto.

I think men want the variety but will never walk away from a voluptuous bouncy big girl. There are gripping points with a big girl. There is a ride with a big girl. There is the excitement of being trapped in the grasps of big thighs that even a body builder may not be able to escape. There is the idea that a big girl would be in control. Little, diet-worshiping women are often small on top, do not have much warmth, may be frail to a fault, and are usually bitchy! There are entire dating Web sites that are for big girls, and I don't know of any dating sites that are exclusively for the skinny.

These big girls, including really big girls, often reveal exactly what they want. First, they usually need a man with a big unit, for the lack of a better word. They will say, "I am big and curvy and need somebody I can feel." They express that if you are a big guy, two big bellies make for difficult coupling. These girls are very good at getting their intended pleasures made clear, "Because I'm big, this does not mean my sex games do not include intercourse." I had conversations with big girls who emphatically stated their case and were very choosy about who they may agree to meet. That should tell you something about the popularity of big girls. They can be selective because there is no shortage of willing men.

I tried to pursue one such large lady, who described herself as obese. I told her she was what I liked and that my imagination had me already excited. I miscalculated how happy I thought she would be to hear from me. My approach was pretty bold, and she projected, in graphic language, what she wanted done and what she could do back.

It ticked her off! "I got back; I'm not just a piece of meat you know. I'm a lady and I want to be treated like a lady. Is this how you treat all your ladies when asking for a date?" Now, this lady's written presentation was full of distinct, detailed descriptions of every sex act that I could ever imagine, and the popular terms for body parts and suggested activities were used throughout. My answer could have been, "No other lady has ever talked to me like that before." There was some request for every orifice of her body and directions for use. I was taken aback and found myself apologizing and trying to save a communication with her.

This lady provided photos of herself that left nothing for the imagination. The cumulative effects of the dirty talk with graphic words and pictures gave me the feeling it would be tough to go too far in my response. But I did, and with all that I have described, she was more than willing to send me off, never to talk to her again. That did not sound like a hard-up woman.

Three days later, she wrote me an e-mail, of which I don't recall the contents, but it resulted in further dialogue. She asked for a picture of me. I did not include one for view of everyone on this Web site to see me. Discreet is a frequently used word, though I did wonder how discreet those many people insisting on discretion could be, as they supplied a picture of themselves for the Internet-browsing world to see.

After I considered who I was talking too, I sent a picture, a bad picture of myself, sounding very eager to please her by agreeing to all her stated requests. She told me basically to hit the road. And that was it; she never tried to contact me again. Now, when you take into account that I had some success with women who were very good-looking in every way, it is clear that, firstly, there is someone for everyone, and secondly, fat does not prevent women from finding suitors.

Next, I spoke to a sixty-six-year-old cross-dresser that showed himself in fishnet stockings and a black miniskirt with white panties. Exactly provocative! He explained he was a bottom guy (submissive), and I played to that with an initial contact that I hoped would titillate him enough for a response.

The first thing I told him was, "I'm going to throw you over my shoulder and take you wherever I want and do whatever I want." So dialogue commenced. I further discussed how I would lower his panties and spank him. He got the picture and admitted that excitement was creeping into him as he thought about it, and he said, "You would not have much of a problem with me." He then stated his weight, light for a grown man. He was not short but skinny. My profile listed my size, which is large, and my appearance, which I've been told is intimidating in terms of a physical man.

I implied that I was bisexual and had female partners strong enough to perform these rather physical tasks. I told him I had a midforties bodybuilder woman who could manage my 245-pound frame and whip me upside down with my legs over her shoulders. I said she was five foot ten and weighed about 175 pounds, plus she was quite attractive.

The guy was exchanging e-mails with me every half hour and asking to arrange a rendezvous and for directions to the location. He said he was willing to reward this woman. I told him a lady like this one would accept rewards, but her participation was for the sexual satisfaction she gets by dominating and dangling a man in a helpless manner. (I might add I had not yet actually found a lady dom offering this kind of service.) I now had to start to back off and out of this correspondence, as I had gotten this rather elderly gent in a frenzy over a scene I couldn't deliver—unless he wanted a man, which I believe he would have accepted. Naturally he wanted me to drive the six hours to his place or vice versa, and he requested that this session would take place a couple times. I told him I'd think about it, and it's been months since I've communicated with him.

The interesting feature about this incident is that a homosexual male was lured out of that for a chance of having a sexual encounter with a female. No hesitation; whatever it took to create that submissive, slavelike experience, he was willing to do.

This brings us to the nontechnical, nonexpert point of views of genetics versus choice regarding homosexuality. Bear in mind that I do not care if you are homosexual or not, and I believe you are entitled to all privileges afforded straight people. Having said that, I truly believe that being gay is more a matter of sexual preference than a genetic component of that particular human being or that a genetic difference is the driving force of his or her sexual preference. I think the very front-and-center purpose of this gay issue is political, and the best argument for gays to gain all the same rights as straight people is the genetic issue.

Maybe the focus on gay people's sexual behavior is way overdone. The sexual behavior of any adult is nobody else's business. And maybe the gay community has brought the emphasis of their sexual behavior on themselves. There is much flaunting of their romantic feelings that is too public, which would be true of a straight couple carrying on too affectionately in public.

As I went through these Web sites, the presence of male on male and female on female, either paired or grouped indicates a willingness to indulge in a homosexual act. It is just as gay if two men are in different parts of a lady, as is true if it's two ladies and a man.

By the descriptions in their profiles, the desires of these couples are talking about interaction amongst all the parties when they refer to observing while the other man or lady does things with the other partner's spouse or friend. The excitement of viewing your spouse taking part with another party of either sex is gay. If you insist on your partner getting it on with another of the same sex or if you are observing to your pleasure another party of your own sex, you are gay!

As illustrated with a couple of examples of people profiling themselves as gay or bisexual, it's possible to lure them out of their stated behavior to the alternative. Forbidden behavior is always exciting to many. A man who normally prefers sex with women who perform sexual acts that could be duplicated by a man is a candidate for a homosexual moment.

The only normal straight-sex requirement is traditional intercourse, where a penis and a vagina are required.

Everything else can be accomplished by like partners. Speaking for myself I have never had the desire for anal activity in either position, but I do enjoy the oral stimulation. There is a difference between being the receiver and not the provider. But if you provide oral sex for a same-sex partner, you are definitely gay.

Consider the S&M scene, where it's all about pain and humiliation and choices between being submissive or dominant and having male masters or female dominants and male or female submissives and sometimes slaves. These are possibilities for what excites a person most. Choosing, for sexual purposes, male or female partners has everything to do with what excites an individual most. The true issues concerning being gay is the right to shared medical benefits, the ability to legally raise children, and the ability to live with each other with no detriments to their freedoms—the same freedoms enjoyed by the straight community.

One rather elderly lady, in her early sixties, just wanted to be spanked on her bare bottom. She was clear that she had no other interest; she wanted a mature man to take her, scold her, lower her pants, and spank hard, to the point of welts and serious reddening. She wants to cry like a small child. As unbelievable as it may sound, I came across that request a number of times. And there are men that like only to spank bare bottoms. This lady couldn't make it any more clear that she wanted to be spanked hard and long, then left unable to sit down, but she did not want to be touched in any other way. In her picture, this lady showed her ample backsides with a close-up, not revealing anything more than this rump, displaying the bent-over-the-knee look.

With this particular case, I became somewhat of a cupid, as I had communicated with a spanker and now a spankee. The problem was that both members were over sixty, and they were 1,500 miles apart. I do not know that it was beyond the extent anyone might go to if the excitement takes over enough. I think such extended efforts do occur for the sexual high! I did pass on the user names of both parties to each other. The spanker told me her picture excited him tremendously. I do not know if there was a happy connection for either of them.

I always got turned away by dominant men, with one exception. I communicated with a 350-pound, six-foot-four dominant male who was only about one hour from my home. He listed his age at thirty-three. He was lots younger than me, 100 pounds heaver, and six inches taller. He outmatched me in every category. I decided to be cautious; I've watched the WWF. Communications got frequent and closer together. That is a sign of intensity, and he was graphic about what he was going to do and how excited he was getting. That was the very last I heard from this guy, even though he had worked himself up in an eagerness to get this on. Again and again this happened. Male doms wanted nothing to do with me—after leading me into conversations about the activities and the idea that they were drill sergeants and I would be terrorized to displease them in any way.

One exception, maybe, was a large, possibly twisted type of guy that looked like Grandpa on *The Munsters*. He was tall, and by the picture he looked large-framed. After a couple exchanges, he said he hosts these activities in his specially designed chamber at his home and once you are in and he's underway with his routine, there would be no turning back. This was a signal of a possibility that I had already been considering, and I believed a warning was being issued about his own self-control. I have to say that his appearance was the deciding factor in my decision not to push this further. If I felt this way, there is room for everyone to feel that way when a situation looks a little scary.

I left the SMBD scene and went back to sexually expressive sites looking for partners. Many of these ladies show a private part of their body and then describe themselves as wanting to be treated as a lady. This confuses me a bit. Not saying this to be funny. It was difficult to know what kind of response she was looking for. Remember, I've traveled the sites that are not sexually explicit (standard dating sites). Women on these sites might hint they are not prudish and have words like eroticism to politely let you know what their thinking is in that regard. I think any lady looking to date knows full well that mature dating couples should expect sex to eventually be a factor. I further believe that if that is very unimportant and you are not interested in that part of a relationship, you should make that known to avoid wasting time. You may be with somebody incompatible.

Individuals whom have little to no interest in this part of the relationship would be wise to let an inquiring prospect for a date know, as most people seeking partners are at least somewhat interested.

By most First World nations' standards, we have hang-ups regarding sexuality. I think we bring our children up in a disciplined society that implies that sex is wrong. Parents talk about the importance of saving oneself for the "one and only," so as not to be spoiled goods. This may be the morally correct route, but I doubt it's mentally the best route. With small children you may say whatever you want, because until they have an interest in sex, nothing is much affected. You could be talking about calculus to attract the same inattention from a child. It is more serious when a child is becoming aware of sex as he or she is exposed to it. The question of who a child should approach with these questions becomes a dilemma.

I was a freshman in high school when I began to take interest. And I could rely on juniors and seniors in high school to show me what was really what! I already had a wild imagination and was making up all kinds of stories at age fourteen. Up to this point, I had not seen a girl my age or older undressed. However, I had stories to match my classmates' and the upperclassmen's stories—all nonsense, untrue, and probably silly.

There was, however, a pretty serious interest in being informed and included. I did not know terms commonly used to describe sex acts or activities or even how to pronounce body parts I was unfamiliar with. You could always find the kid that's got a magazine with great pictures or in my day, the French playing cards, which showed detailed images of women's bodies and were about the only pictures that did so. They were the best, as the early *Playboy*s were less revealing, focusing on upper body and rear-view nudity. Don't get me wrong; Hef is still my hero today!

Well, I was seeing things I sure was interested in but had no idea of the science involved in such a complicated issue. For some reason, I didn't expect to see all that hair there and I wondered just exactly where what I was looking for was. There are not many places or people to seek information from. There has to be a trust involved— that no one is going to tell anyone what you are asking about and that your lack of any knowledge will not be laughed at.

Parents didn't seem to be a good idea, as I'd been punished for playing doctor or looking at a naughty picture, such as the Sears underwear ads, which were still of some interest from time to time. I could not imagine my mother or father informing me of this subject. When I was in school, the health teacher was the basketball coach, so that would have caused some complications. The family pastor—I don't think so. In the end, one half hour of difficult discussion occurred between me and my mom. Hats off to her trying to be a good mom, but like all moms the ideas of a "special one" and "love" were emphasized as guidelines for whom to engage with someday, but she was not much help in explaining how and why! What I learned,

I learned from the guys, in rather crude expressions that I'm sure led me to inappropriate conclusions.

There appears to be less restrictive attitudes regarding sex everywhere else, excepting countries dominated by their religions. Religion here in America is a major reason for our attitude here. The country is predominantly Christian, Jewish, and Muslim, all Bible-affiliated religions. Although the testaments of the Bible are distinctly different between the religions, many of the books, history, and figures are the same. From the beginning, a link between sex and sin was either stated or implied. Story after story guides us through all the wrong things, the holy message of how sex is supposed to be. Bible readers know a lot of rules were broken by people who paved the way for those religions. The characters of the Bible do not practice what is preached in it. I am not scolding the Bible for the contradiction, and I firmly believe a spiritual life is a more rewarding life. But the Bible is the most influential force in the world. It denounces sex in many ways, so followers attempt to please the Lord with "acceptable" sexual behavior. Parents want their offspring to do the same.

I fundamentally disagree with the church, preaching their interpretation of the biblical direction concerning sex. It is hard to connect what the church preaches and how the human being naturally functions. The church of course has long thought sexual intercourse to be only for reproduction purposes. Yet the male of the species becomes aroused daily, from eleven years old until death. Often more than once a day this urge pops up, and boys and men engage in masturbation to relieve the urge, even if it only does so briefly.

It is apparently true that women generally need something to spark those urges, and that does occur. Modern young women express sexual desires almost equal to those of their male counterparts. I'm told the solution is the same. So, applying some logic here, the sexual appetite is either a natural gift or a God-given gift because it is an explosively strong feeling that drives some people to behavior inconsistent with their conscious thought processes.

To stop in the middle of doing the laundry or pruning a tree to seek gratification is an abnormal function, and it's very likely your day's plans did not have this on the schedule. And if you are somebody going through puberty with little frank advice, being told to leave yourself alone or you'll go blind has never been the helpful answer. So parents, church, school, and any other power figures during your adolescence are not often helpful.

The procreation argument conflicts with the volume of semen a healthy man can produce. I'm not referring to the swimmers; I'm talking about the semen released one to three times a day, every day, for sixty-five years or more. This is far too much for procreation purposes. If every time a man ejaculated a new life was started, we'd be well into water shortages, never mind energy and land. And if you ladies are not totally aware, the orgasm of a man is the few seconds of ejaculation. The time spent getting there is very pleasant also, but it culminates in the release of semen. Let me remind you, this is not to say that a good God may have created us this way, but the church, through biblical instruction, is adverse to a climax for any reason other than procreation. But I'm not sure of the God that the Bible tells us about. I have considered that there is one, and he's better than the one described in the Bible; he may not be perfect and may not be all powerful or omnipotent. And I think that if he exists, sex was a gift to be enjoyed often by his creation.

The biblical doctrine that is hurled at us is to limit the intended enjoyment of sex, and it refers to sinning every time sex occurs without a sanctified partner, before a sanctified partner, or after a sanctified partner. I believe temptation is a natural occurrence and that a shutdown does not occur when viewing or considering forbidden property. You have a special and great relationship when that sex for love goes on with the same vitality forever in your marriage or any permanent relationship.

So let's throw jealousy into this discussion, as this is no doubt the big obstacle for sex beyond a married couple, as well as the vows! These include the woman vowing obedience to the man, and that obedience theme is echoed in the Bible all the time. A disobedient woman is in dire straights according to biblical lore. The twenty-first-century woman is anything but not equal to a man of this century. The Bible has a commandment that deals with adultery and coveting another's wife. That, in fact, calls the women a piece of property, not to be touched by anyone but her sanctified partner. The same protection is repeated in the commandment that does not prohibit the man from taking part in sex with another women not belonging to another man. There appears to be a double standard. Adultery is described as vow breaking, because sex is not prohibited by biblical doctrine in any way if you are not married, unless, of course, you are female. Stoning as punishment for this did occur, according to the Bible.

"Thou shalt not covet thy neighbor's wife" had much to do with jealousy. As women were treated as property, the rule "Thou shalt not covet thy neighbor's goods" makes the former redundant. But it is jealousy, a normal human emotion, that causes violence even today because of third-party interference in romantic relationships. I do not see any solution to jealousy that results from such an intrusion. But it is acknowledged in the Bible and has become one of the biggest rules. So one might conclude that wedding vows have exaggerated the sin of jealousy through the exclusionary rules regarding sex with anybody other than sanctified partner. This has exacerbated an already hurtful human emotion.

I do believe the Bible is a basic rulebook, created with the intention to control a society. It is entirely written by men who were dealing with the specific problems of those times. The poor and indigent were flung into the streets—yet, "honor thy father and thy mother." Life was not precious, and crimes against humanity were well documented—yet, "thou shalt not kill." The ideas of spiritual celebration of traditions that encourage love, family, hope, and charity are what make for a better life. Spirituality should be honored, but the Bible is not to be taken as the literal word of God.

Brothels and houses for sex are contrary to the moral fiber of this nation, which still roots itself in Christian doctrines. However, higher regulations regarding such places create problems that more passive societies need not deal with.

Compare the rate of sex crimes in the States with the rates of other European countries, in which the regulations are more relaxed. The startling fact is that concerning sex crimes in First World nations, we are ranked number one. In every category, we lead the world with sexual predators, and there has to be reasons for that. We spend lots of tax dollars on prosecuting sex crimes that are not violent and involve consenting adults. Prostitution to support drug habits, of course, has to be put in check, but prostitution to earn a living? And, especially for those who have no other way to connect with a partner, being a patron of prostitution is hardly a crime worthy of committing police, legal, and corrections resources; this is overkill. The government needn't endorse it, but it should be decriminalized and perhaps loosely regulated, for health purposes. However, as far as the potential for disease, I can almost guarantee that safe sex practices are better observed in this service than the bar scene.

I further wonder how many marriages may have been screwed up because husbands and wives have grown into the attitudes that obstruct a healthy view of sex. In this research through these Internet pairing sites, I have found that people who are sexually stressed—horny—become that way if a partner is unwilling to move on, through the years, to new and different sex activities. Sameness makes it difficult for some people to push the libido, and signs of disinterest and an inability to perform develop. If a husband can no longer reach a satisfactory result with traditional intercourse, some change may work, and that change can come from his regular partner. This of course is true for either partner having trouble with satisfying sex. Both parties must agree upon and be willing to try what might rejuvenate the excitement. Boundaries can be sources of interference, which is why it is necessary to ask for the new practice as well as ensure the willingness of the partner to provide it.

If a couple goes to bed agreeably and the man becomes impotent in traditional intercourse, there are different positions, activities, or body parts that can be used. However, if either party is unwilling, there is a problem that will likely evolve into something bigger. You trace such boundaries back to family upbringing if the lady finds the request to be dirty, to be unnatural, or to degrade her in some way. This works the same when a man refuses to try to satisfy the lady.

It seems the problems with the less sexual and more sensible matchmaking services are largely related to finding the right partner. This is not as neat as the advertisements sound, and membership will not always produce a match.

Testimony after testimony finds one of the partners unhappy.

Matchmaking, I'm convinced, is a very difficult business. We all have an idea of what we want in a partner and that could be as various as we have numbers of people. There is an ideal that cannot be found by eye and hair color, height and weight, ethnic and racial features. Body type is another vague area as there are multitudes of shapes and sizes. Pictures can tell lies or be misleading. But many men find themselves scanning through the pictures, stopping to check the profile of a lady that interests him initially because of her picture. The reverse is true also, but women put less emphasis on looks, generally. Personality traits are next, as compatibility is going to rely on similar interests and possibly a similar demeanor. This is why trying to match someone is difficult; the other method of making pairings is through people known to each other already.

A smart lady wants to meet on her grounds with her rules. A smart man would know that, but it is common that this consideration isn't given. It's common, I believe, because of the number of men using these dating services who lack confidence. It's easier to understand why a woman turns to these services, because it's hard to make your availability known.

Once the profile is popped up, there are key areas a guy might be looking for to maintain his interest. For most men, sexual interest becomes a first—or at least an important—element. Some ladies answer certain questions by giving an impression of sexual interest that can be interpreted as casual, unimportant, important, or enthusiastic. It may be a sad fact for some women to hear, but by a wide margin, men want enthusiasm in that area. So if the lady is also enthusiastic and implies it, even in a subtle way, she is going to get more calls than the lady who expresses a negative view. It's best, if you are not too interested in a sex partner, to leave that as a mystery.

A women is likely to read the profile and consider a man's appearance after liking what she has read. She is very often looking for independence with a suitable partner who has his own means to relieve a financial situation or at least improve on it. She does not need a partner to burden her that way or sponge off her. I have, however, found that some women are influenced by a man's look even after his profile has peaked a lady's interest.

I have two pictures that I would only send over on personal e-mail, not post on a dating site. I had one good picture of me that would pass as not very good-looking and one other that is okay enough. With some dialogue, I can usually figure out the inquiring lady's financial situation. All of my serious correspondents were people in at least their middle fifties.

I portrayed a retired man not too worried about having funds to live with, and I implied my new partner would not have to remain employed unless she wanted to. The partners in need of some financial support or supplement would accept my picture, no matter whether it was the good one or the bad one, with little change in our situation. Ladies in no need of or concern regarding finances took me off their contact lists! When I portrayed myself as getting by, I was nearly always abandoned. My conclusion here is that a man can generate more interest if he can project financial stability; good looks are not the biggest factor. However good looks become more useful with financially independent women. So unfortunately, but not surprisingly, a good-looking woman and a well-off gentleman are the most sought after for relationships. Both would also have healthy sexual appetites. It is an issue!

On the gay scene, the priorities are not the same. Looks seldom seem to be an important issue. When I portrayed myself as a gay man, most responders were primarily concerned with loyalty and sex. The sexually explicit dating gay sites were most entertaining, as the men do not leave too much to the imagination. One-night stands are not discouraged on these sites, and it seems like a measure of compatibility is ascertained from these occasions.

I did not find a serious male gay site that was not somewhat sexually explicit. I did not successfully gain entry to a lesbian Web site. I further did not consider someone to do that for me, as I wanted to be sure that I was witness to anything contained in this book. But I do believe that with gay men, sex is the number-one issue. You cannot make that comment true for every gay male couple, but my communications with a hundred or so men indicates that this seems to be the situation by a majority. I have the feeling on the lesbian side the sex is very important but not exactly as it is with men. Women make more loyal and trustworthy spouses for each other, and that it is very important for females; therefore, the emphasis on sex is slightly less important.

Now, I find this to be revealing, as the other important concerns for life are secondary. We know that straight men and women find sex important but not overwhelmingly so. I know that on the dating services for gay men it is indeed the deal maker. I communicated with several prospective dates for a gay partner. The conversation was always pretty frank about sex acts and my preference. It seemed to me to me that if you would allow another man to have intercourse in what is imagined to be the most common way, you were going to have at least one date.

Distance didn't even enter into the conversation. You could get a partner to travel many miles for a rendezvous. Sometimes finding a male sex partner if you are a closet gay man is extremely difficult. You can't just jump into a conversation with a question about someone's sexuality. And the gay bar club scene is not where closet homosexuals are. So it does not take long after an initial hello for gay men to start migrating to the sex talk. It appears to me that two gay guys will live in undesirable conditions if the sex is right, whereas two gay women want a normalized living atmosphere. To me, this difference shows that genetics is not that big of a factor; it has more to do with the choice in partner than sexual preference!

Here is the most interesting description I could find regarding the SMBD lifestyle. I find SMBD an odd behavior trait. It involves humiliation or creating the humiliation to reach the height of excitement. Much of the humiliation comes from forced sex or perceived forced sex. Real pain and pretend pain are prominent, as I have had discussions covering this part of the act. Face slapping and spanking are the two most common and easiest applied methods.

People want their fannies reddened. And pictures and testimonies of pleasure on these sites confirm a willingness for serious, welt-producing behind lambasting. Some like it best delivered by a dominant female, and some don't care if it's a female or male. They want to be exposed and beaten well. Some of these people do not even mention the need for sexual encounters of any kind beyond the dangling over someone's lap and getting whipped. Indeed, I have had dialogue with people who expressed that very want: Beat me and do not service me in any other way. And doms have said, "If you visit me, all you are getting is the discipline, you will not touch me nor will I touch you in any sexual way." I have considered that language to be a legal disclaimer, but I have done enough interviews that this is the real deal for many.

The diaper lady, the spankers, the torture and pain administrators are not doing more than that. There is mention in different ways that being rewarded for good service is appreciated to necessary in some cases. But many potential clients that detect that hint are turned away, complaining that the motivation is wrong. It is a strange thing, humiliation for excitement.

One submissive male, thirty-three years old, described his best experience to me as I portrayed myself as a dominant male interested in adding clients. He said I couldn't match what he had going for himself right now. He is serving a husband-and-wife team of doms. He'd been there once and was hoping they would call him back for another session. Those were their rules, and they may never call back! I asked, "What do they do?" He was instructed to come to their home and ring the doorbell and enter the old-style Victorian home. He would be buzzed in. Once he was inside, he would find a folded paper with instructions under a ceramic vase. The instructions told him which door to enter and to strip to his underwear and wait. The room was large, with a bed, a large table, and a trunk. Mirrors were everywhere, including the ceiling.

After a few minutes, a forty-five-year-old female entered the room in a black negligee and boots to above her knee. You could not see any of her private parts, as a solid black bra and black panties were being worn under a netted upper garment that draped to just below her waist and was lined with a black hem.

She grabbed him by his mouth and led him across the floor and ordered him to kneel and keep his eyes fixed on her. He did. She was taller than him, five foot eight, and blond. She carried a thin twenty-inch whip. He looked into her eyes for thirty seconds, and then she slapped his face four times in a row with her right hand. On the fifth she faked a slap, and he flinched, so she slapped him twice more. She ordered him to lie prone on the floor. He complied. She removed his underpants and placed her pointed-heel boot on his rump. She asked him if he thought it necessary to cuff him. He said he'd rather not be cuffed and said he would do whatever she wanted.

She told him to reassume the kneeling position but to stare right at her pubic area. He did, and she moved to within an inch of his face. She asked if he would like some of this, and he said yes! She said, "You're not getting any of it." She grabbed the back of his head and she pulled it to her, just touching his face. She ordered him to extend his tongue, touching her panties in front. She asked if he could feel her shape underneath. She held his head there for a minute. Then she swiftly leaned over him and demanded he put his hands together, and she cuffed his hands behind him, telling him she would do whatever she wanted.

She put him back with his tongue on her panties again for another minute. He said he'd never been more excited and started to beg for her to touch him or let him at her. She remained holding him like this for another two minutes.

Then the husband, who was imposing as a big bearded man, very muscular and rather hairy, entered the room. She exited and was not to be seen again.

Now this client was naked, extremely aroused, a bisexual, and handcuffed and in the hands of a large, dominant B&D, sadistic male. He did whatever he wanted to, whatever your imagination allows you to think, for about a half hour.

I asked if he ever reached satisfaction, and he indicated that at the point of a serious spanking, he was stepped on by the male, and he masturbated. That was the session-ending act.

The dominating male told him his clothes would be outside the door of the room. He told him to dress and leave and to not mention the location, or he would never be called. He said they would call him for a return visit and that months could go by before that happened.

This client believed the female was watching his servicing her husband by some means, closed-circuit TV or a peephole. But he would pay a hefty fee for a repeat session. He said the hottest part was her holding his tongue on her, telling him he would never get a look at her. He didn't! And this client said he was never asked to contribute in any way, but he had experienced a couple that appeared to be in it for the highest sexual excitement, and they provided that for him.

That would be the ultimate satisfaction from the intention of that type of matchmaking site. So the question is, where does that leave our society, where the tradition is man and woman as sex partners for forty or fifty years? How do the statistics measure up with the numbers of people indulging in sexual behavior as just described? Are there many marriages or partnerships in which the loss of that zip in sex has been the cause of destroyed lives? How much dialogue occurs regarding a married couple's loss of sexual appetite? It is very hard to express such details frankly to your life's partner. So it goes without being discussed, unsolved, and unresolved.

It is not abnormal for these sexually deviant ideas to enter your psyche. But hasn't your sense of decency and your upbringing forbid any resolution to approach these problems? I think it does and the causes should be discussed, in the hope that better private and personal conversation can turn this around for better, healthy sex in marriages and with long-term partners.

A good first step into sex authorities is to question what is "legal." We all seem to agree that sex is something for mature human beings. For many years, eighteen-year-olds have been of legal age to engage in sex without being arrested for child molesting. That seems sensible to me for that argument, but I wonder about laws where both parties are sixteen. These are of course consenting sixteen-year-olds, and for that matter, consenting people down to some predetermined age should probably be decriminalized. Anyone being forced into a sex act is a victim, and we should retain the laws that punish that kind of predator. Sex has to be consensual for it to be okay under any circumstance, for any age, in any kind of relationship.

It would be projected by responsible parents that sex ought to be held off for mature people who understand what's going on. Common sense should be a factor when determining whether a crime is being committed. Two consenting ten-year-olds is a bad thing, though I doubt it should be an arresting offense. A ten-year-old forcing his or her way on somebody else is a crime, particularly so if it's a younger or weaker party. This is obvious wrongful sexual aggression, and the laws should reflect the severity of the crime itself.

I can't see how sex between two consenting adults can be a crime in any way! Soliciting sex for money is hardly a crime, as it is consensual; the solicitor likely needs the money and the solicited likely wants the sex. There's no rational reason why these two can't have that. Standing on a street corner is not appealing in any neighborhood, so each town could have rules against public solicitation. There should be a private manner of either seeking or providing sex. This may not be morally good by most people's standards, but it should not be illegal.

I believe the legal taboos are all related to religious convictions, because I do not know of any major religion that has looked at sex and sensibly ignored it as none of their business. Those influences have come from the role religion has played in history, and the lawmakers of those times were stricter and more afraid of their clergy putting unnatural restrictions on this normal human function.

I dare say sex-related misdemeanors are handled differently in Oklahoma City than in Philadelphia or Boston based on geographical philosophical differences. Haven't we all watched *Cops,* when they shackled and knocked solicitors and the solicited to the ground in the name of crime prevention and public protection against such dangers? However, substance abuse and sexually transmitted diseases have to be controlled, so you cannot endorse a society of free-roaming sex.

When an arrest or detainment occurs, the severity of the crime ought to reflect the nature and the features of the incident. A recent sensationalized story about a seventeen-year-old boy being incarcerated for an assault crime on a consenting sixteen-year-old girl showed an absolute abortion of justice!

The educational system has been perhaps the most rational of influences in a counseling role. Adolescents need to be informed of the choices that go along with sex. Parents who believe the "Just say no" solution are blatantly ignorant. Parents, with very few exceptions, are not going to be the source of advice from a questioning and maturing child. In progressive educational systems, the information is generally accurate with precise, clear explanations.

I think most males are less concerned with answers and more concerned with involvement with a girl. Girls, with much more at stake, are nervous and confused as to how they should be handling this issue. So in plain English, parents interested in protecting their daughters should be totally supportive of their children receiving good sexual information from their schools. The other big factor is parents who think that growing up today is like what it was when they were growing up. The pressures on youth to fit in with the crowd appears to be much more of a concern, and being unpopular these days is a more serious issue. There's too much emphasis on looks and being on the "inside" and having a boyfriend or girlfriend.

Then you have an ever-advancing gay movement. Like it or not, it is a lifestyle choice that is here to stay and will infiltrate and impact life everywhere in the United States. My research, nonscientific but relying on common sense, shows that the gay population is expanding and becoming less of an issue in more and more places. My personal take on that is there is a little gay in all of us! It is just totally irresponsible of parents to not provide protective resources for potentially sexually active young people.

I am an advocate of a more liberal sexual attitude, against government and religion trying to impose restrictions on a gift nature provided and which authority figures have used for power plays and have been grossly hypocritical regarding.

The most conflict between sexual attitudes and authority figures is with the clergy and people's religious convictions. This is a tough issue because having beliefs is very important to get through this life with some comfort and hope. I understand the amino acids and spark theories, DNA, and all the brilliant study to bring about tremendous progress in finding the "how" but still come up short with the "why." Much of the Bible echoes other ancient mythology, Greek and Egyptian amongst them. The writers could have put a favorable spin on women and sex if they chose to do so. But they didn't, and women have been a condemned creature in our world throughout Bible lore. Sex, staying with the same spin, had to be a bad thing except for when making babies. But the facts regarding whether we are here by design or accident has little to do with our sexuality. I believe that most humans find sex very pleasurable, unmatched by any other natural human expression or experience. I fully recognize that some people do not, for one reason or another, feel that way.

Other than the Virgin Mary, who was demoted from the Holy Trinity, almost all the other women were responsible for the biggest sins. The only other woman of favorable mention, however precarious, was Mary Magdalene, first introduced as a prostitute. The Bible is full of devilish women, all of whom are created in scripture and offered up as factually historic figures. In some Bibles there is a predecessor to Eve, named Lilith, who fought with Adam in a power struggle and became exiled from the Garden of Eden. She was rumored to be devilish, roaming the desert and defiling men she came upon and luring them into her control sexually.

Religions have the right to project a moral standard, and they should leave it at that! There are laws that prohibit the most heinous sex crimes, and a little threat that you will receive no spiritual reward if you commit such crimes is sensible. This is now no more than a moral issue, as government has—rightly so—not made consensual sex illegal.

Any entity espousing restrictions or repression of sexuality is defiant to the natural desire of our human species.

Whether we are of divine creation or an accident of nature the sexual part of us was intended for frequent pleasurable occasions.

The point being the tremendous ability to have this gift is being poorly served by religious and moral authorities for interference between consenting adults.

Those choices by nature should be left to the individuals.

There are many reasons for adultery. Adultery, by definition, is sexual intercourse between a married person and someone other than his or her spouse. Intercourse is defined as copulation. By the letter of *Webster's New World Dictionary,* the former president may not have lied about the kind of affair he had with young women in the Oval Office. It's admittedly a stretch, however.

While I'm not endorsing every mature human to freely move about seeking sex without an awareness of any potential fallout in their life, I am suggesting that relaxing the intensity of the issue long ago would have perhaps saved a lot of failed marriages and prevented much crime. I would be surprised to find very many Catholic schoolgirls and other strongly Bible-bred females to have shed that fear of God following them around.

Then there is the long-married couple whose sex has become something short of zesty. Even open communication between the couple, sharing what each needs to stay enthused, is prohibited. The husband would not say to his wife of forty years, "We need to try new things to keep me interested." There are new things and untested things that most couples don't get to do. Many men have girlfriends because they do what the wife won't do! This is entirely true for women too. I feel, however, that it's the man that falls into this quandary most often. Losing sexual interest in a partner is likely a natural situation, but there is help available to spice it up and save the heartbreak of possible betrayal. A couple with healthy sexual regularity has the best chance of evolving into new acts that provide the satisfaction that could be lost. However, it is dangerous to stop sexual interaction for an extended period and then try to start it up again. The communication gap has increased, and what worked seven or ten years ago is likely to fail.

The Internet dating sites and the specialized sites reveal an interest in expanding our sex lives. They are a modern example of how we think. The idea that the people on these sites are not a fair sample of all of us is false. As time moves on, the freedom to express is more available and personal identity is somewhat more protected. So people hoping to get as much missed sex in before they can't anymore. A younger generation is there also, as the female has climbed into equality, expressing desires that prior generations did not dare to.

The gay scene is, in my estimation, much bigger than first thought. Not a lot of men thirty years ago would have dared say they were gay, but I have found men that say they are not gay involve themselves in threesomes where two members are male. If you're counting them, there is a greater ration than, say, 1 in 10. Women appear to be more gay, even. And I think that with women it's a lot more than a sexual issue. I think a it's little sad to say, but most men have had an easier life, and many women see another woman in a spousal role as more agreeable and equal.

Some of the sexual fetishes described do not make these people weird, just unusually aroused by different fantasies that are not generally talked about. It's an uncommon man who expresses sexual satisfaction from being spanked or dressed as a baby and diapered. Women have been happy to show servitude in unconventional, humiliating circumstances. This just means that such people are no longer excited by the traditional sexual role. So I think these sites are not doing any harm to anyone and have a purpose, showing that it is normal for many people to feel like this. By a very large margin, both men and women want to serve someone. Some do not expect gratification and do not demand it. They want to be the provider and must get some satisfaction out of being denied.

People on these sites are from ages eighteen to eighty, well educated and well employed. Sex is to be a most powerful act and not intended to be restricted or regulated when two consenting adults are involved.

In the interest of fair play I corresponded with a submissive female, pretending to be a dominant male interested in expanding my harem. I asked her to describe her best experience. She said she had liked her visit with a female dom who was the spouse of a male dominant she'd had a date with. After or during a training session involving restraint, the wife showed up unexpectedly and appeared to be shocked as to what was going on.

The woman entered the room dressed like she had just come home from shopping. She was ranting and raving realistically enough to scare the submissive guest. She started in on the insults and asked the client, "What do you think you're doing?" The dominant male was asked to leave the room and told that he would be dealt with next. He departed and looked worried.

She described the woman as tall and athletic-looking, as if she regularly worked out, and she appeared to be more fit than her husband. This submissive client was petite and all her limbs were bound. The wife took over, demanding the client take part in a wrestling match with the woman, with a serious attempt to pin her as she undid the bindings. The woman stripped to her underwear and then proceeded to wrestle and soundly thrash the submissive subject into several wrestling holds, causing multiple orgasms for the client.

The true submissive had believed she was in a real submissive situation, which took away the staged, role-playing mentality, and the excitement she'd felt was unmatched by anything she'd ever done before. Of course, this was in fact a planned act for the client, but she was not clued in on it until it was over. The lady told me she fell all over herself thanking them for the experience, though of course it couldn't be the same again because she would know the next time that it was all staged.

It is interesting how popular it seems to be to become the weaker or even helpless individual when it comes to sexuality. There are dominants, and I think the male dominants are in fact aroused by their actions, but so many more men express a preference for being a submissive, and it is very exciting to them.

The female dominants that I have had some dialogue with often expect a reward, and I think there is some excitement for submissives at receiving financial demands from their doms. This is a good deal for the dominant one if he or she can get away with it. So I think there are those that weed out the candidates who are unwilling to pay before they get too far into setting up a date. And I maintain that when rewards are expected, you will not receive the best service from this performer.

The Bible's condemnation of sexual activity reminds us that the authors of the Bible and recent clergy have denied any notion that Jesus might have had a girlfriend or wife. However, applying logic to the stories of Jesus tells me he may very well had a female companion that he loved. All accounts of Jesus tell a story of a very interesting and attractive figure, by his appearance and his words. This is perhaps the most famous man that ever lived, and in his time he was not loved by everyone, and he was a threat to some because of his reputation alone. I believe Jesus did exist and was a magnetic powerful speaker/preacher and was the hope for many of the world. Some of the stories connected to Jesus might have been embellished or exaggerated by writers of the New Testament to influence Christianity. It is not difficult to believe that Jesus had a mate and that they enjoyed all the pleasures of human love during their lives.

Because religion is based on blind faith, there could very well have been stories of him raising a family for a period of time, believed with the same certainty. There is nothing to prove Jesus's life was as it was written, and there is nothing to prove his life was vastly different than what is written, except that the notion that Jesus was human enough to be sexual and loving in that way would not have sold well with a body of people trying to set a standard that would degrade women and make them seem inferior to men. The theme is constant throughout the Bible, and the male writers of the scripture continue on and on to discredit most any female in biblical history.

There was fear that Mary the Virgin Mother could become the most revered figure in the Bible because of the Immaculate Conception. But she is quickly dismissed, and there is very little mention of her after the night of Jesus's birth. You can easily connect the religious view of women and sex to a threat to the church's absolute discipline.

The Christian God that I spiritually celebrate has tasks to do that are beyond the human imagination. And in the twenty-first century it is hard to sell blind faith as the answer to the very difficult questions. We are, by and large, a rational society trying to make living a rational experience. The monotheistic religions seem pretty willing to credit our God with all that is good, but he bears no responsibility for the things that are bad. If a tornado blows through a neighborhood and a survivor proclaims he was saved by God, he must be blessed, but across the street, an elderly couple perished—who must, I suppose, have not been blessed. I contend that if there is a great God, there would not have been a tornado in the first place. The boxer that credits God for his knockout victory over his apparently godless opponent, never gets on the microphone and blames God when he is defeated. I think we are holding God to a human standard and not a deific standard. All these things could be cleared up if God would make an appearance and let people know he couldn't possibly control everything or hear billions of people's prayers all at the same time.

Then of course you have the stories of spectacular and often unnatural events in the Bible. When you admit to yourselves that these are old stories that have made their way through the thousands of years with the purpose of creating rules to live by that made sense only at that time, you can see that the Bible is not to be taken literally. It is for good and order that religions helped people to be charitable and kinder to each other. It levels the playing field somewhat for the people with less to manage, with the better-equipped folks, to get through the trials and tribulations of life.

I find comfort in the belief that Jesus did exist and was a very important preacher of goodness and kindness. A good God would certainly be happy to have a human promote goodwill and charity to our fellow man. As modern times have revealed so many truths that are contradictory to ancient Bible stories, why haven't the churches taken steps to be the guardians of mankind and represent the best qualities for a good life? Much of their resentment of this commonsense approach is a hesitation to relent that our forefathers might have been wrong regarding the Bible as the "word of God." A lot has changed, and things keep on changing, forcing the church to either go along with those changes or steadily fall back. The church would have more chance of survival if it operated as the spiritual leader of all people, without the need to drive their beliefs down the throats of people who are not willing to accept it as gospel. One would believe it's just a matter of time before the doors of many of these faiths will close due to a lack of finances. On the limited occasions I go to church, I've noticed that the pews contain less and less people. The most telling measure is the declining attendance at Christmas services, which traditionally bring out the most members. In my own Christian church, it's appalling how much attendance has fallen off in just the last five years. If you take away people over fifty, there would only be a scattering of folks in the pews.

The idea that Jesus suffered for all of us can still carry weight, as I'm sure the Romans wouldn't have been tolerant of a populist preacher building a following as he argued the virtues of kindness and the best qualities of human beings. There are a number of theology students that could rewrite the Bible or even produce a new holy book that is more fitting to the times. I cannot emphasize enough that people want to believe and would value the comfort of a religion that relied less on miracles and more on substantial tangible assistance.

I think the driving concern is the promise of heaven and the redemption of all of our sins. We all are sinners, according to the Bible, and by its standards, I dare say most of us probably are. But I know a few folks that are so good, in their work for humanity in general or just in surrounding themselves with such people that they could not be sinners. No one knows what occurs after death. That is a fact; it is absolutely undeniable. People hope there's a beautiful place where we are reunited with everyone we want to see again and we are all free of our human frailty. Of course I wish that to be the case, but I think the odds are against that happening. I think it's just an absolute end of the life and existence of an individual. That means that there is no disappointment to be felt at not ending up in heaven.

Considering there was life on this planet before I ever arrived, I can't dismiss the possibility that you come back as somebody new to do it all over again. I couldn't guess whether you may come back as a goose or a mosquito or born into human royalty. I can't overlook the possibility that you could be a creation somewhere else in the universe. And through all of this, there may be a God that keeps things going. He or she is a good God by giving us the resources that support life, keeping our species alive. A good God would see the turmoil we've created for ourselves and could maybe tweak our intelligence to overcome the greed and dishonesty of man. I have always thought ignoring the environment and building destructive weapons would be our demise, caused by our own ignorance. We now know what should be done to protect these vital resources, and if we do not do anything to help ourselves, our demise would be poetic justice. It would make sense for us to ensure our future generations have a safe place to live, and we might just be helping ourselves if we do revisit this planet, which is equally as possible as every other guess regarding our afterlife.

Notes

Notes

Notes

Notes

Notes

Printed in the United States
by Baker & Taylor Publisher Services